Farmyard Friends

GOATS

Maddie Gibbs

PowerKiDS press.

New York

Published in 2015 by The Rosen Publishing Group, Inc.
29 East 21st Street, New York, NY 10010

First Edition

Editor: Caitie McAneney
Book Design: Katelyn Heinle

Library of Congress Cataloging-in-Publication Data

Gibbs, Maddie, author.
 Goats / Maddie Gibbs.
     pages cm. — (Farmyard friends)
 Includes index.
 ISBN 978-1-4994-0137-0 (pbk.)
 ISBN 978-1-4994-0139-4 (6 pack)
 ISBN 978-1-4994-0134-9 (library binding)
 1. Goats—Juvenile literature. 2. Domestic animals—Juvenile literature. I. Title.
 SF383.35.G53 2015
 636.3'9—dc23
                              2014025285

Manufactured in the United States of America

CPSIA Compliance Information: Batch #CW15PK: For Further Information contact Rosen Publishing, New York, New York at 1-800-237-9932

CONTENTS

Goats are farm animals.
They live in **herds**.

Female goats are called does or nanny goats. Male goats are called bucks or billy goats.

Baby goats are called kids.
Mother goats have
one or two kids at a time.

horn

hoof

A goat's feet are called hoofs. They have **horns** on their head.

Goats eat a lot of grass. Farmers also feed them hay and grains.

Farmers raise goats
for milk and meat.

Goat hair can be brown,
black, gray, or white.
It can be long or short.

British alpine goats have short, black hair. They make good milk.

Angora goats have long hair.
People use the hair
to make **yarn**.

You can see goats at farms or petting zoos!

WORDS TO KNOW

herd

horn

yarn

INDEX

WEBSITES

Due to the changing nature of Internet links, PowerKids Press has developed an online list of websites related to the subject of this book. This site is updated regularly. Please use this link to access the list: www.powerkidslinks.com/fmyd/goat